Dedicated to Chris and Karen, Casheena, Cretia, Craig and Laura, Kevin, Rachel, and Chris. We each produce fruit in our lives; whether bitter or sweet, it is there for the world to see. Always strive to produce the sweet fruit, as it will bring joy into your lives continually.

THE FRUIT OF THE SPIRIT

A Study of the Character and
Nature of the Holy Spirit

PIERCE MOBLEY

Halo ●●●●
Publishing International

ISBN: 978-1-61244-376-8
Library of Congress Control Number: 2015951493

Printed in the United States of America

Halo ●●●● Published by Halo Publishing International
Publishing International 1100 NW Loop 410
Suite 700 - 176
San Antonio, Texas 78213
Toll Free 1-877-705-9647
Website: www.halopublishing.com
E-mail: contact@halopublishing.com

ACKNOWLEDGEMENTS

I want to give thanks first to the Lord who shared these teachings with me many years ago. I also wish to thank my wife Pam Mobley, who is the first to read and hear the words I write. It is through her that many ideas and thoughts are brought into greater clarity. Many thanks to the adult Sunday school class at The Alley in Gainesville, Georgia for their support and prayers. I also want to say thank you to Jodie Greenberg for her editorial insights, and to Lisa Umina and the entire staff at Halo Publishing International for their hard work in bringing this book to print.

TABLE OF CONTENTS

INTRODUCTION

As a new believer in Christ and excited to study the Word of God, I was eager to learn and experience all that the Bible had to give. It was during one of those times of study that a Scripture seemed to leap off the page at me. I had come to the close of 1 Corinthians 12 when verse 31 reached out and grabbed at my heart: "But covet earnestly the best gifts: and yet shew I unto you a more excellent way," (KJV). Though the words were written to those in Corinth in the first century, it seemed as if the old apostle Paul had written them just for me.

In my passion and zeal for these greater gifts, in April of 1994 I filled a backpack with some clothes, water, a tent, sleeping bag, Bible, and notepad, and climbed to the top of Black Mountain in Suches, Georgia to be alone for three days in search of the greater gifts. What I found in that time of fasting and prayer was the more excellent way that the Apostle Paul desired to show me. Thus began my desire to see the fruit of the Spirit produced in my life and the lives of others. It is by the fruit that is produced in our lives that we are known to the world, and those greater gifts come through the fruit.

CHAPTER 1
THE VINE AND THE BRANCH

John 15:5
I am the vine, ye are the branches:
He that abideth in me, and I in him, the same
bringeth forth much fruit: for without me ye can do nothing.

Standing among the grapevines along the gently sloping hill to the Garden of Gethsemane just outside of Jerusalem's walls, Jesus reached out towards the thick, twisted grapevine rising up the trestle that supported its weight and held the branches up off of the ground. Looking intently at His disciples with whom He had shared the previous three years, He declared, "I am the vine." With this, not only did Jesus indicate that He was the center of their lives, but also that He would become the *source* of their lives; He—like the vine—would be their anchor.

To begin any study on the "fruit of the Spirit" we must first understand the relationship of the vine and the branch. This relationship is the very basis necessary for the development of the fruit of the Spirit in a Christian's life.

The vine is the very foundation of the branches; it is the strength of the branches, and it is the source of life for the branches. Without the vine, there would be no branches, and subsequently there would be no fruit. The vine and the branch each have a responsibility to one another. This interrelationship must be maintained in order for fruit to develop and mature so that it will have the full capacity to change our lives and the lives of others with whom we come in contact. One needs only to look at a vine and its relationship to the branches and vice versa to see the similarity between our relationship with Christ and His with us.

So what exactly are the responsibilities of the vine and the branches to each other? The vine is the branch's very life, and the branch is completely dependent on the vine for its life and its security. By the same token, the branch is responsible to bring forth fruit. The vine never bears fruit of itself. Look at a fruit vine or tree and you will see that neither the vine (nor trunk), nor the limbs ever blossom or bear fruit. They must have living branches in order to bring forth fruit. The branch is what reaches out the farthest from the vine, and produces the fruit which reveals the vine's. It is through the branch that fruit will come. A healthy branch will produce an abundant amount of fruit.

The vine must give life to the branches and supply the branches with nourishment. The vine's roots, deeply implanted within the rich soil, draw nutrients and water from the ground and send them into the branches. A grapevine then produces sap (its lifeblood) that flows into the stem, and either one or multiple grapes develop on the end of the stem. This fruit identifies the vine. The sap flows through the center of the vine within its heartwood and out to the branches. The branches open up to allow the sap to flow through their heartwood and then into the stem of the fruit. This sap nourishes not only the branch and gives it life, but it also nourishes the fruit.

Just as a vine pours its life into the branches, Christ has been poured into us by the Spirit. The Apostle Paul gave us the picture of Jesus living through us in Galatians 2:20: "I am crucified with Christ: nevertheless I live; yet not I, but Christ liveth in me." What is this life-giving sap that flows from Christ (the vine) into the believers (the branches)? It is the Holy Spirit. Jesus told those with Him that He would "pray the Father, and He shall give you another Comforter, that He may abide with you for ever," (John 14:16). The Holy Spirit flowing into the believers gives them both life and nourishment.

The vine also must be firmly rooted deeply in the soil to give the branch a strong, stable foundation from which to cling so that when the winds and storms blow, the branch will be secure in the vine. Christ is our foundation, just as the vine is the foundation for the branches. It is a strong foundation that cannot be moved; we are anchored in His hand. Jesus affirmed that through Him a believer is held in the Father's hand, and no one is able to pluck a believer from His hand (John 10:28-30).

Now that we understand the relationship of the vine to the branch, let us examine it in a broader sense. An abundance of vines and branches creates a vineyard. Every vineyard, in order to be healthy, has a caretaker, or husbandman, that watches over the vineyard to see that it is productive. Our heavenly Father is that caretaker, always looking at each branch for both the quantity and quality of fruit being produced.

Jesus speaks of three types of branches—in John 15: the first, unproductive; the second, producing some fruit but not of good quality or quantity; and the third, producing much fruit by abiding in Jesus.

First take a branch that is not producing fruit the scripture says will be "taken away" (John 15:2). While this verse gives an image of the branch being removed from the vine by the caretaker—God the Father—that is not what it means. The word used in the passage for "taketh away" is the Greek word "airo," which means to be lifted up.

Take the case of a branch in a vineyard that is not producing. It has fallen down to the ground, only to become covered in dust and dirt. Lost in the shadows of the other branches, this branch does not receive enough sunlight to produce fruit. In this case, the caretaker will lift it up, gently wash the leaves, and place it somewhere along the trestle where it will be in the light. If needed, he will support it by tying it up until it becomes strong.

This is what our heavenly Father does as He looks to and fro among the living branches and sees one of us who has fallen down into the shadows. He will lift us up, wash us off, and then bind us up in the light until we are strong again. Ask yourself, why would God remove us from the vine when we do not bear fruit, when Jesus said in John 10, that there is no one who could remove us from His hand.

Oftentimes believers fall into temptation, become discouraged, or fall into despair, lost among the shadows and becoming covered in the dirt and mud of circumstances. It is then with a gentle hand that the Father will begin to cleanse the wounds of life and wash away the guilt or shame of failure. Then, with loving hands, He will lift them up to a place where they find rest, reassurance, and healing, and become strong again in the light.

Secondly, there are those who are fruitful to an extent, yet their branches are growing more than they are producing. In a vineyard, branches that grow uncontrollably produce few grapes. All their energy is spent on growing and not being productive; their fruit is weak. These branches will need to be pruned, or "purged" (John 15:2). The process of pruning in a vineyard is to focus the branch on its purpose and to also prepare the branch for the coming spring rains. Pruning takes place during the winter, a season of rest for the branch. When the branch is pruned it will lift up towards the sky in expectation of the coming spring rains, with the excess growth having been removed.

Those who bear such weak fruit among us are the believers who are going in all directions or working in ministry with no real direction. In churches all across the world, there are people who are using a large amount of energy being involved in all kinds of activities and ministries. They may be bearing some fruit but are frustrated in their walk. These are the ones for whom the vinedresser is coming with the pruning shears. Too often our problem is that we try to resist the pruning shears, thinking that we can't give up all of these responsibilities; yet, it is what is needed in order to concentrate our growth in the proper direction. It also allows us to experience the refreshing rain of the Holy Spirit rejuvenating our relationship with Christ.

Lastly, the most productive branch is the branch that has learned to "abide" in the vine. When you go into a vineyard and look at where the branch connects to the vine, you will see that some are very wide at the base compared to the other branches. These branches receive the greatest amount of life-giving sap compared to the others. These are also the branches that produce the highest quality and quantity of grapes.

The believers who have learned the principle of abiding are the ones that seem to excel in ministry no matter where their ministry is. The great mystery for many is defining just what "abiding" is. I too have had that problem of wondering just what it is to abide. I found the answer in a little book written by Bruce Wilkerson entitled *Secrets of the Vine*. In this book, Wilkerson defined "abiding" as the place where a believer understands that it is more important to be with God than to be working for Him.

Too many of us are stuck in the second area of weak growth because we are too determined to define the depth of our relationship with God by how much we are doing for Him rather than by how much time we are just spending with Him. If we look at the example of how Jesus was abiding with the Father, we can understand the power of just being with the Lord.

Scripture reveals how Jesus would rise up early and go off alone to pray (Mark 1:35), how He would pray in the evenings (Mark 6:46), and how there were times that He would even pray all night (Luke 5:15). His times of abiding (of being *with* the Father) focused Jesus on His purpose, and in turn He was productive. The ability of Jesus to abide in the Father prepared Him for the greatest test of all, and that was the cross.

The branches will always reveal what kind of vine or tree of which it is part of by the fruit it produces. Thus, since we as the branch abide in Christ, the world should be able to identify that we are Christians. Jesus said:

> "Ye shall know them by their fruits. Do men
> gather grapes of thorns, or figs of thistles? Even
> so every good tree bringeth forth good fruit; but
> a corrupt tree bringeth forth evil fruit. A good
> tree cannot bring forth evil fruit, neither can a
> corrupt tree bring forth good fruit. Every tree
> that bringeth not forth good fruit is hewn down,
> and cast into the fire," (Matthew 7).

Which vine does the world identify you by—the true vine that produces good fruit or the vine that produces evil fruit? This study of the fruit of the Spirit will reveal to us whose vine we are branches of.

POINTS TO PONDER

1. How does the relationship between the vine and the branch reflect your relationship with Christ?

2. That are the three responsibilities of the vine to the branches? How is this similar to the responsibilities that Jesus meets in His relationship with you?

3. What is the responsibility of the branch?

4. What is the purpose of the husbandman (caretaker) in the vineyard?

5. Where do you see yourself in the area of growth: non-productive, productive but not to your full capacity, or producing good fruit? What do you need to take you to the next level of growth?

CHAPTER 2
THE FRUIT

Galatians 5:22
But the fruit of the Spirit is love, joy, peace,
longsuffering, gentleness, goodness, faith, meekness,
temperance: against such there is no law.

Every fruit shares nine traits. Apples and grapes, oranges and peaches—all have these nine traits common to each other. If you take any fruit and slice it you will discover each of these characteristics. There is the stem, the skin, the aroma, the texture, the taste, the meat, the core, the juice, and the seed.

In Galatians 5, the Apostle Paul exhorted the followers in Galatia to produce the fruit of the Spirit and not manifest the works of the flesh. What do we know of the singular fruit of the Spirit? Have we examined the fruit of the Spirit? How does this contrast with the works of the flesh?

According to Galatians 5:19-21, the flesh produces seventeen various works, including: adultery, fornication, uncleanness, lasciviousness, idolatry, witchcraft, hatred, variance, emulations, wrath, strife, seditions, heresies, envyings, murders, drunkenness, and revellings. Paul warned that those who practice such things would not inherit the kingdom of God. In fact, Paul is using a stark contrast between the many "works" of the flesh and the singular "fruit" of the Spirit. It is by using this contrast that Paul is able to get the attention of the readers of this Epistle. Whereas the flesh produces many works, the Spirit produces a single fruit—yes, single.

However, many would say that there are differing "fruits" of the Spirit in nature, and it must therefore represent nine separate fruits. For instance, 1 Corinthians 12:4 states that "there are diversities of *gifts*" (emphasis mine), with nine gifts of the Spirit listed in 1 Corinthians 12:9-10. This indicates a plural meaning. Yet, how many fruit trees or vines have we seen that produce more than one type of fruit? Do apple trees produce oranges? Does a grapevine also produce a pear? The answer of course is *no*. An apple tree produces apples and an orange tree produces oranges.

However, Galatians 5:22 describes the *fruit* of the Spirit in the singular. Is not the wine a gift that comes from the grape? Isn't the jelly a gift that also comes from the grape? How many different gifts come from a single fruit? This conception provides a stronger contrast to the *many* works of the flesh than do multiple fruits. One fruit with nine characteristics, when matured in the believer, will reveal the very nature and character of the Lord and His Spirit within that believer. Thus the Holy Spirit only produces one fruit, not many fruits.

Given a single fruit of the Spirit, let us compare that fruit to the works of the flesh. A work of the flesh is a product of our emotions. Sexual immorality, rivalry, jealously, and anger are all works of the flesh and are all products of our emotions. They are reactions provoked by outside stimuli, received by our five senses, and then acted upon by the passionate desire to ease a particular emotion. In other words, the works of the flesh are a reaction to a particular outside stimulus that triggers an emotional response.

In contrast, the fruit of the Spirit is developed from within the Spirit of a believer as a result of being led by the Holy Spirit over a period of time. To illustrate, let's take a farmer who plants a vineyard. The vines must be nurtured and developed over time in order to produce branches that produce fruit. This is the same with the fruit of the Spirit. At our born-again experience we become branches. Our development as branches over time allows us the opportunity to produce fruit pleasing to the touch and taste. We develop over a period of time, drawing life from the vine. We allow the vinedresser to work on us, cultivating our growth through prayer, experience, and the Word until our fruit matures, bountiful and sweet, drawing others to desire the life within.

Conversely, the works produced by the flesh never satisfy. Look above at how Paul lists these works. He groups sexual sins together, and these sins become progressively more depraved as one produces the next. Each work of the flesh tries to satisfy some emotion; yet, as each work manifests, it brings a person down a new path of depravity until these works completely destroy them. As it says in Proverbs 13:15, "The way of the transgressor is hard."

So, not only is the way of the one producing the works of the flesh taking them down a dark path to eternal punishment, but the path of the flesh is also a hard road to travel. It is full of disappointments, hardships, and dissatisfaction—the inability to be truly satisfied deep inside, simply treading into the judgment of God and towards eternal separation from Him.

Paul says that if we are led by the Spirit we will not fulfill the works of the flesh. We will produce the fruit of the Spirit against which there is no law. There is no law of man that would make this fruit illegal. There is no law of God against those who produce the fruit of the Spirit in their lives. How comforting is it that there is there no law on Earth or in heaven written against those who produce this fruit in their lives. As opposed to the hard way of a transgressor, the path of a believer will be one of reward and contentment.

The fruit that we bear will reveal the vine to which we belong, thus revealing our identity. Natural fruit is produced over time by a biologically controlled process that is determined by the seasons. The spiritual fruit that is produced from within us is also produced over time through the seasons of life until it has reached maturity and is ready to be plucked and consumed by those to whom we minister.

Now that we better understand the fruit of the Spirit, we will be examining the characteristics of natural fruit in context with their spiritual counterparts:

Natural Fruit	Spirit Fruit
Stem	Love
Skin	Joy
Aroma	Peace
Texture	Longsuffering (patience)
Taste	Gentleness
Meat	Goodness
Core	Faith
Juice	Meekness
Seed	Temperance

POINTS TO PONDER

1. How does Paul use contrast to teach the fruit of the Spirit?

2. How many works of the flesh does Paul name?

3. How does the one fruit relate to the nine gifts of the Spirit?

4. What is the root of the works of the flesh? How are these works triggered?

5. How do the nine characteristics of the fruit of the Spirit relate to the nine traits of natural fruit?

Chapter 3
The Stem-Love

1 John 4:19
God is love.

The stem of a fruit does two things: first, it supports the fruit, and second, it supplies life to the fruit while it grows. The stem is an extension of the branch, which in turn is an extension of the vine. The stem is what reaches beyond the branch. It carries within its confines the life of the vine to nourish the fruit as it develops, but the stem is also what supports the fruit. If the stem fails the fruit fails, and the vine cannot be revealed to the world. The stem of a fruit is its point of support between itself and the branch, and it is also the one thing that reaches out beyond the branch.

To understand the stem we must understand the nature of the vine. Just what is the nature of the vine? How is it defined? How is it identified? What is the nature of Jesus—the vine—given that the Holy Spirit reveals to us that He is the Son of God? It is the very nature and character of God that is being revealed to the world through the believers.

What is the character or nature of God? What one characteristic defines God and compels Him to reach out to a fallen world? Picture a balance with its two cups hanging off the end of a bar, which in turn is fixed to an upright support. The arms of the balance are our neighbors (reaching outward) and are affixed to the vertical support (our reaching up to God). These two are held together and balanced by "love," the pivot point of all Scripture. This element of love describes why God reached out to a lost and dying world. John 3:16 says that "God so loved the world, that he gave his only begotten Son, that whosoever believeth in him should not perish, but have everlasting life."

Jesus, when asked what the greatest commandment was, replied in Matthew 22:37, it was to love God with all your heart, mind, soul, and strength; the second is that we are to love our neighbors as ourselves; that all the law and all of the prophets hang upon these commandments; and that love is the anchor of everything—the pivot point of everything for the believer.

Let's go back to our balance. The first thing that has to be in order in our lives is our vertical relationship between the Lord and us. It is when we love God with all of our being that we are prepared to fulfill the second most important commandment, and that is to love our neighbors as ourselves. The one emotion that drove the Father to reach out to a lost humanity was love. The one action that drove Jesus to the cross was love. The one action that compels us to extend ourselves to worship and love God with all of our being and to reach out to others should be love. It is love, for without love there is no mercy, forgiveness, or compassion for those who are lost or in need.

To engage with others out of love, we must first understand and define love, and then we must understand the results of ministry without love. 1 Corinthians 13, or "The Love Chapter," guides us in the definition of love and gives a focal point, or motivator, for ministry:

What Love Is	What Love Is Not
Suffers long	Does not envy
Is kind	Does not boast
Rejoices in truth	Does not want its own way

Bears all things	Is not irritable
Believes all things	Is not resentful
Hopes all things	Does not rejoice at wrongdoing
Endures all things	

As we see, the first characteristic of love is its ability to endure suffering. How many of us have been deeply hurt emotionally? How many of us have loved ones who are not serving the Lord and we carry the burden for them in our hearts? How many of us endure injustices inflicted upon us by others? Do we get upset? Do we blame God or get angry? This answer is often "yes," yet Paul says that love suffers long without complaint. Love is kind, never looks to hurt, but always looks to serve, to make another's life better. Love is befriending those that others reject, helping a stranger in their time of need, and always looking to perform simple acts of kindness. Love finds its joy in truth—both in speaking truth and listening to truth. Love seeks truth. Love draws its energy from truth.

Love is never envious. Love doesn't care what others have or how God may be blessing others. In fact, love will rejoice for the good that others receive. Love does not boast; it serves without a need to be recognized. Love always yields to others, never seeking to have its way. Love is gentle; it does not get irritable, even under great stress. Love does not resent, but instead is content in whatever situation arises. And lastly, love never rejoices in wrongdoing. Love never seeks nor relishes the wrongs that may befall someone; it is grieved by any wrongdoing.

Love is able to bear hardship and it believes all things. It hopes in all things and endures all things. The true test of love is that when life seems to put weights of care upon the soul, it believes that things will get better. Love will always look to hope, even when others have given up. Best of all, love will endure.

True love weathers the storms and is made stronger by never giving up or giving in. The Apostle Paul emphasizes that love always looks to the needs of others, and its greatest desire is to serve others with the goodness of God. It never looks for any type of reward. Love does not obligate or manipulate!

When reaching out to the world we must be motivated by love. The fruitlessness of a ministry without this awesome force of love is revealed in 1 Corinthians 13:1-3. These verses demonstrate that whatever we do in ministry (outreach), if we do it without love, we do our ministry in vain.

> "Though I speak with the tongues of men and of angels, and have not charity, I am become as sounding brass, or a tinkling cymbal. And though I have the gift of prophecy, and understand all mysteries, and all knowledge; and though I have all faith, so that I could remove mountains, and have not charity, I am nothing. And though I bestow all my goods to feed the poor, and though I give my body to be burned, and have not charity, it profiteth me nothing."

Imagine having the ability to speak any language of any country and also to speak the language of angels. To have this ability would make you a standout among men and a great missionary. Someone who could relate Scripture to anyone would benefit people greatly by promoting the Gospel. Yet, Paul said that if one could speak in both the tongues of men and angels but did not have love, they would be broken cymbals. Theirs would be an irritating sound to the ears of God.

If we have the gift of prophecy, the knowledge to understand all mysteries, and have faith to move mountains but do not have love as the focal point of outreach, then we are nothing. All of that knowledge and faith would be wasted as though it never existed in the eyes of God. Imagine bankrupting yourself to give to the poor and you are rendered completely penniless. Imagine surrendering your body to be burned for the Gospel but not being motivated by love. The Scripture says it will not profit you one bit. If we are not motivated by love to reach out to others, then we are ministering in vain; the Lord will not even recognize our efforts.

Ask yourself, are you reaching out to others because of love, or are you motivated by something else?

POINTS TO PONDER

1. What are the purposes of the stem? How does the stem relate to love in the believer's life?

2. What is the central point to which all things are balanced?

3. In defining love, how does your life compare to the characteristics defined by 1 Corinthians 13?

4. What does someone become when love is missing in his or her ministry?

5. When you examine your heart, what motivates you in ministering to God and others?

CHAPTER 4
THE SKIN-JOY

Nehemiah 8:10
For the joy of the Lord is your strength.

As noted in chapter 2, the skin of the fruit is associated with joy. The strength of the fruit of the Spirit is the "joy" of the Lord. But why? How do you define joy? To begin to understand these questions, we must understand that the skin is not the nutritional strength of the fruit, but instead it is what holds the fruit together. The skin protects the fruit and its tender interior. The skin also determines when the fruit is ripe.

When the hot sun is bearing down upon the fruit, the skin protects it and keeps it from drying out. When the storms come and the rain beats down upon the fruit, it is the skin that protects the tender goodness within from bruising. When the winds blow hard and stir up all manner of dirt and dust, it is the skin that protects the soft fruit within from becoming soiled. The skin wraps the fruit and gives it strength to endure all the hardships of the field while it develops. The skin also shows that the fruit is mature and ready for harvest.

Many times joy is mistaken for happiness, and many Christians become discouraged when their individual experience as a believer isn't a continual wave of euphoria. Often, when temptation or hardships of life arise, these burst their "happy" times, and the hot fire of tribulation destroys their experience.

There is a very distinct difference between joy and happiness. Happiness is determined by circumstance while joy is based on contentment. *Webster's Dictionary* defines happiness as "a pleasurable or satisfying experience." *Wikipedia* defines happiness as "a fuzzy concept and can mean many things to many people." In short, happiness is determined by positive experiences or circumstances. In fact, there is an entire subdivision within the psychological sciences dedicated to researching how to maintain positive circumstances—both physical and emotional—that boost happiness.

Joy, however—especially the joy of the Lord—is not determined by circumstance. According to *Theopedia*, an online theological dictionary, joy is "a state of mind and an orientation of the heart. It is a settled state of contentment, confidence, and hope." Joy is based on contentment, not circumstance.

The Apostle Paul wrote in Philippians 4:13, "I can do all things through Christ which strengtheneth me." We love to quote this Scripture but neglect the previous two verses that really tell us of the depth of Paul's relationship with Christ which reveals to us where his strength comes from: "Not that I speak in respect of want: for I have learned, in whatsoever state I am, therewith to be content. I know both how to be abased, and I know how to abound: every where and in all things I am instructed both to be full and to be hungry, both to abound and to suffer need," (Philippians 4:11-12). In order to fully understand the depth of Paul's suffering here, we must look at 2 Corinthians 11:23-27:

> "Are they ministers of Christ? (I speak as a
> fool) I am more; in labours more abundant, in
> stripes above measure, in prisons more frequent,
> in deaths oft. Of the Jews five times received I
> forty stripes save one. Thrice was I beaten with
> rods, once was I stoned, thrice I suffered ship-
> wreck, a night and a day I have been in the deep;

In journeyings often, in perils of waters, in perils
of robbers, in perils by mine own countrymen,
in perils by the heathen, in perils in the city, in
perils in the wilderness, in perils in the sea, in
perils among false brethren; In weariness and
painfulness, in watchings often, in hunger and
thirst, in fastings often, in cold and nakedness."

Paul's strength was not determined by his circumstance. His strength was in his ability to be content in his heart no matter what, and he received his strength through a settled heart and focused mind. He learned how to be abased (brought down low) and how to abound. He understood what it was to be full or hungry, to abound or suffer. Paul stated in Philippians that he could do and suffer all things. Why? Because it was Christ who strengthened him. His knowledge of the power of Christ was the basis for his joy, and Paul understood that joy came through obedience.

Jesus gave us the greatest example of joy in action when He suffered the cruelty of the cross. Hebrews 12:2 says, "Looking unto Jesus the author and finisher of our faith; who for the *joy* (emphasis mine) that was set before him endured the cross, despising the shame, and is set down at the right hand of the throne of God." What was the joy? It was in the satisfaction of His complete surrender to the will of God and what it would perform for fallen men. Jesus looked beyond the circumstance and into His hope.

It is our response to circumstances that will prove if the joy of the Lord is working within us or not. Joy is our strength; it is not just a mindset, but it is also a covering for us. The joy of the Spirit not only strengthens us as we endure hardship, but it also protects the tender places of our inner man.

If we compare all of Paul's hardships to those in modern America, could we still love God? The end result of his outer circumstances, though harsh, did not affect the inner tenderness of his heart. As described above, he suffered five beatings with whips; a stoning; three beatings with rods; three shipwrecks (a day and night in the sea); frequent journeys; perils of waters, robbers, and heathens; and perils in cities, in the wilderness, at sea, by his own countrymen, and among false brethren. He also suffered in weariness, in painfulness, in hunger, in fasting often, in nakedness, in frequent watchings, in thirst, and in cold.

It is from all of these outer sufferings that 2 Corinthians 27 illuminates the true character of joy. It says that what mattered most was the "care of the churches." Paul was less concerned for his own well-being than for his burden to the churches.

Horatio Spafford was a successful businessman in Chicago in the mid to late 1800's. He had a warehousing and shipping business along the docks at Lake Michigan. He was married and had one son and four daughters. In 1871 he suffered the loss of his son, and the Chicago fire wiped out most of his warehouses. He was nearly ruined financially.

In 1873 Spafford had planned a much-needed European vacation for his family. A week before they were to leave, he was detained by urgent business. Sending his wife and daughters ahead—telling them he would catch up with them in London—he turned his attention to concluding his business. Several days later he received a telegram with the simple message, "I alone saved."

The ship on which his wife and daughters were traveling was involved in a collision with another vessel, and all four daughters had perished. Spafford quickly sailed to England to join his now grieving wife. While sailing in the Northern Atlantic—about two-thirds of the way across—the captain of the ship knocked on his stateroom door. Escorting Spafford to the deck, they stood amid ships along the port rail. The captain told him that they were not sure of the exact point at which the ship sank, but this was the general area. There Horatio Spafford stood, staring down into the black, cold waters of the North Atlantic under the starlit sky. Pulling his cloak tighter around his shoulders, he quietly slipped down below to his cabin.

Once inside, he sat down at the small writing table, and there in the flickering light of an oil lamp, he penned these words:

> When peace like a river attendth my soul,
> When sorrows like sea billows roll,
> No matter my lot
> Thou hast taught me to say
> It is well it is well with my soul.

Here was a man who had just written one of Christianity's greatest hymns, and it came at a time of dark tragedy in life. If it were not for the "joy" within him and covering him, he would not have been able to stand in the black of the North Atlantic night looking into the cold, dark water that entombed his daughters without becoming filled with the bitterness and anger a grieving father would experience, let alone be able to sit and pen those words that would become the healing salve for his very soul and for countless others.

Joy not only strengthens us for the hardships of life, but it also protects us from the temptations and trials that will ultimately come our way: "Think it not strange the fiery trial which is to try you, as though some strange thing happened upon you: But rejoice, in as much as ye are partakers of Christ's sufferings; that, when His glory shall be revealed, He may be glad with exceeding joy," (1 Peter 4:12-13).

Joy is the visible sign of how far into maturity our inner man is, because it is how we handle the hardest trials of life that reveals how ripe our fruit is.

POINTS TO PONDER

1. What two purposes does the skin serve and how do these reflect joy?

2. What is happiness based on? How does happiness affect our relationship with Christ?

3. How is joy defined? What is the basic characteristic of joy?

4. How is joy expressed in Paul's life, and how is this similar to your life?

5. Do you see a ripened fruit when you face great adversity, or is your fruit still growing?

CHAPTER 5
THE AROMA-PEACE

John 14:27
Peace I leave with you, my peace I give unto you:
not as the world giveth, give I unto you. Let not
your heart be troubled, neither let it be afraid.

A better way to describe "aroma" would be "fragrance." Bound within the fruit is its fragrance, a sweet odor that, when released, initiates the desire to taste the sweetness within. The fragrance of the Holy Spirit is peace, and when its sweet aroma is released it will draw others to the goodness of God that not only delights, but also fills, the soul. The fragrance of a fruit is not released until it is either pressed or its skin is pierced and the sweet fragrance bursts out from within, filling the space around the fruit with the soft, sweet smell of the fruit's soul.

In John 14:27, Jesus says, "Peace I leave with you, my peace I give unto you: not as the world giveth, give I unto you. Let not your heart be troubled, neither let it be afraid." Jesus made a distinct difference between the peace of the world and His peace (notice He said *my* peace). The peace of the world is temporary at best. The world defines peace as the absence of conflict. Yet, we know that in that context the world is never at peace, because whether you have peace between individuals, communities, armies, or countries, peace is based on lack of conflict. It only takes a wrong word or some infraction to break the calm and bring chaos back.

However, the peace Jesus gives us is much like the eye of a storm. The storm is all around us with swirling wind and thunder and lightning, but right in the middle is the eye. The sun shines and all is calm, peaceful. This is how we—being filled with the Holy Ghost—should be in the midst of life's storms. We only need look no further than the very one who said that He gave us His peace to see a perfect example of the peace of the Spirit.

In the final hours of His life here on Earth, Christ gave us the greatest example of what true peace really is: "And the men that held Jesus mocked him, and smote him. And when they had blindfolded him, they struck him on the face, and asked him, saying, 'Prophesy, who is it that smote thee?'" (Luke 22:63-64). Jesus just stood silent as they abused Him and mocked Him. He could have called down 12,000 leagues of angels to rescue Him from all of this and yet He suffered—in silence.

Here, in the judgment hall of Pilate's manor as Pilate questioned Him as to whether He was a King or not, Jesus only answered him respectfully and honestly, and never once did He threaten Pilate with violence or ask to be released. Throughout this back and forth, Jesus would answer softly, and "then saith Pilate unto him, Speakest thou not unto me? Knowest thou not that I have power to crucify thee, and have power to release thee?" (John 19:10-11). Still, Jesus only answered him with a simple statement regarding the origin of Pilate's power: "Thou couldest have no power at all against me, except it were given thee from above: therefore he that delivered me unto thee hath the greater sin."

Later, on Mount Calvary, His battered, beaten, and nearly lifeless body hanging on the cross in painful agony, Jesus was still ministering to others. There was the thief who repented, to whom Jesus reassured would be in Paradise with Him that day. Also, looking to His mother, Jesus wanted to be sure that someone would take care of her. John was given that responsibility, and Mary, from that day forward, went with John and stayed with him until her death.

From the time of His arrest and ultimate crucifixion, Jesus endured it all with peace. He never complained or tried to stop the pain. Jesus could have called down the very angels of heaven to set Him free and pour out vengeance unto all who were responsible for His agony. Yet, He suffered it all with an inward peace, like a fragrance flowing outward, stirring some of the hardest hearts around Him.

Look at the moment when He died on the cross in Matthew 27:54: "Now when the centurion and they who were with him, keeping watch over Jesus, saw the earthquake and those things that were done, they feared greatly, and saying 'Truly this was the Son of God!'" The centurion and those with him were not men known to be overwhelmed with fear or awe. These were battle-hardened men who had been trained to kill until either victory was accomplished or until they themselves were killed. The Roman foot soldier was trained to always move forward, pressing the opposing force into tighter and tighter formation, making them susceptible to the Calvary and its devastating charge. In battle, the Roman soldiers were so well trained that when one fell, they closed their ranks and kept moving forward. Many times these soldiers, especially those in the rear ranks, would literally walk over the injured and dead of their own army because their duty was to continue pressing forward into battle.

Accustomed to seeing death, these same men took great pride and sport in executing judgment. The Romans took crucifixion to a level of cruelty never seen by man before or since. They took great pride in causing the greatest pain for the longest time possible and were insulted when someone did not last more than a few hours. These soldiers would not only gamble for the clothes of those being punished, but they would also wager on who would be the first to die, many times drinking and laughing at the suffering of those on the crosses above their heads.

However, when Jesus died, it was not the Priests or Pharisees who declared Him to be the Son of God. It was not those who followed Him both near and far who declared that He was the Son of God. It was the centurion who—in awe of this one man—declared Him to be the Son of God. This centurion, who had seen a thousand men die a thousand different ways, had watched Jesus die and knew that this man was different, that this man was the Son of God. It was not the *way* Jesus died that convinced him, but it was *how* he died that spoke volumes to this old, hard-hearted soldier of Rome and left him in awe. It was the fragrance of peace that was released when Jesus was pressed and cut that permeated into the hearts of those around Him, like the centurion, and it should also be the same for those who follow Him. 2 Corinthians 2:15 says, "For we are unto God a sweet savour (fragrance) of Christ, in them that are saved, and in them that perish."

We—through all of life's hardships—are to be the aroma of Christ and are to endure our hardships with peace. We only have to look at Acts 7 to see this lived out by one of Christ's early followers, Stephen: "Which of the prophets have not your fathers persecuted? And they have slain them which shewed before of the coming of the Just One; of whom ye have been now the betrayers and murderers: Who have received the law by the disposition of angels, and have not kept it. When they heard these things, they were cut to the heart, and they gnashed on him with their teeth."

Imagine a group of men drawing towards you, wailing and so angry that they are grinding their teeth together on your flesh (which is what "gnashing" is). Those who heard Stephen had conviction so deeply etched into their hearts that they wanted him dead, and that is exactly what they did. Look at verses 58-60, and note Stephen's reaction to the circumstances surrounding him: "And cast him out of the city, and stoned him: and the witnesses laid down their clothes at a young man's feet, whose name was Saul. And they stoned Stephen, calling upon God, and saying, Lord Jesus, receive my spirit. And he kneeled down, and cried with a loud voice, Lord, lay not this sin to their charge. And when he had said this, he fell asleep."

As they were stoning Stephen, he prayed for them with his last breaths and asked the Lord to forgive them their sin and not to lay it upon their charge. Stephen, as he was being stoned to death, was releasing the fragrance of peace, and it was so profound that I believe it was burned into Saul's (Paul's) heart, and he would never forget it.

Even when we are cut with false accusation, backstabbing, lying, cheating, or stealing, it is not for us to retaliate or react with anger, but instead to release the fragrance of peace and seek out ways to live at peace with all men:

Romans 12:18: "If it be possible, as much as lieth in you, live peaceably with all men."

Hebrews 12:14: "Follow peace with all men, and holiness, without which no man shall see the Lord."

It is when life presses us hard with such events as the loss of a job, the death of a loved one, or a sickness—hardships that press us, that crush us—it is then that we are to release the aroma of peace. In doing so, all those near us may be witness to the Spirit that dwells in us richly.

"And the peace of God, which passeth all understanding, shall keep your hearts and minds through Christ Jesus," (Philippians 4:7). When we are able to endure every hardship and every attack of man against us with peace, it draws those who want it towards us; in reality it draws them to Christ.

Remember: The peace of Christ is not the absence of conflict, but rather it is the ability to endure great conflict with calm.

POINTS TO PONDER

1. How is peace similar to the aroma or fragrance of a fruit?

2. How is the aroma (peace) of a fruit released?

3. Why is the world's peace different from the peace Jesus gives us?

4. Define Christ's peace.

5. How do you respond to difficult or stressful situations? Does this differ from the example of Jesus and Stephen?

CHAPTER 6
THE TEXTURE-LONGSUFFERING

Romans 5:3-4
And not only so, but we glory in tribulations also:
knowing that tribulation worketh patience;
And patience, experience; and experience, hope.

When we shop for fruit in a grocery store there are two ways we check for both freshness and ripeness. We either gently squeeze the fruit for firmness—which indicates freshness and if it is overripe—or we thump the fruit, and the sound it makes reveals both its freshness and ripeness. It is the feel of the fruit, its texture, which will either cause us to want it or turn away from it. It is also the same for the believer. Our "texture" is how we "feel" to others, and it will either draw them towards Christ or push them away. Our texture should be drawing them to Christ, just like the fresh fruit always gets picked for the basket.

This, of course, is texture as it applies to natural fruit. Texture as it applies to spiritual fruit is "longsuffering." A better word for longsuffering is patience, and what saint could not use more of that? Longsuffering, or patience, comes through a process. Let me repeat that again so it will sink in: Patience comes through process!

A fruit's texture is gained through process, or experience, in the field. As a fruit develops, it experiences both warm sunshine and soaking rainstorms. It is exposed to both light and darkness. It is through these that the fruit's texture develops to express the ripeness within its skin. The same is true of the believer: We are exposed to various experiences to develop patience that portrays to others the ripeness of the fruit within. How do people respond to you, and how do you respond to others?

We can either exhibit patience or impatience. Patience is defined by the *Oxford Dictionary* as "the capacity to accept or tolerate delay, trouble, or suffering without getting angry or upset," while being impatient is defined as "having or showing a tendency to be quickly irritated or provoked, or restlessly eager." The difference between these two is like the difference between sandpaper and silk. Which of those would you prefer to have for bed sheets?

People who are impatient are like sandpaper: they are rough, irritable, and pushy. They cannot stand delays of any kind, nor do they tolerate people who are slow or irritating. Most impatient people want things to work for them. Some of the most impatient people are those on a highway who see that a lane is closing down in a mile or two, but they stay in that lane regardless until the last moment when they swerve back into traffic, without regard for the safety of others, and causing the flow of traffic to come to a complete stop.

Think about someone you know who is impatient. How many times do they get themselves into trouble due to their inability to wait? Look at people in financial trouble. If you dig deep enough, you will find that they prefer to borrow to gain material things for their lifestyle rather than save and wait to pay cash. Impatient people in the workplace either trample over others to push themselves up the corporate ladder, or they will quit a job and rush off to another one, trying to obtain the position and prestige they feel they deserve. When hard times come, many of these same people find themselves on the street because of their lack of loyalty and self-serving attitude.

A great example of impatience in the Bible is found in 1

Samuel 13:1-7. Here we see that Jonathan, the son of Saul, has attacked a garrison of the Philistines and has overcome them in battle. The Philistines then gathered their army that—according to the Scripture—was as numerous as the sand of the sea. The people followed Saul trembling, like knees knocking, and their stomachs were all knotted up. Saul and the people waited for Samuel the Prophet for seven days, and their fear was making them impatient, especially Saul: "And he [Saul] tarried [at Gilgal] seven days, according to the set time that Samuel [the prophet] had appointed: but Samuel came not to Gilgal; and the people were scattered from him [Saul]," (1 Samuel 13:8).

So what does Saul do when the people start scattering? They were already hiding in caves and holes and in trees. In verse 9, Saul builds an altar and then commands people to bring him the sacrifice and peace offerings. And he offered the burnt offering. Then guess who shows up? Yep, Samuel:

> "And it came to pass, that as soon as he had
> made an end of offering the burnt offering, be-
> hold, Samuel came; and Saul went out to meet
> him, that he might salute him. And Samuel said,
> What hast thou done? And Saul said, Because I
> saw that the people were scattered from me, and
> that thou camest not within the days appointed,
> and that the Philistines gathered themselves
> together at Michmash; Therefore said I, The
> Philistines will come down now upon me to
> Gilgal, and I have not made supplication unto
> the Lord: I forced myself therefore, and offered
> a burnt offering," (1 Samuel 13:10-12).

Saul was so impatient that he did not wait for the prophet Samuel to come and offer the appropriate sacrifices, so he did what was not his duty or responsibility to do. When confronted about his impatience, he tried to explain away his inability to wait for the word of God (a prophet in the Old Testament represented the Word of the Lord), and by waiting he would ensure Israel's victory even in the face of an overwhelming enemy force. What I really like is how at the end of verse 12, Saul says that he had to *force* himself therefore and offer a burnt offering. He had to force himself to be impatient! But no he didn't; Saul's character flaw of impatience was his undoing. Samuels's response to Saul's impatience is classic. Look at 1 Samuel 13:13-14:

> "And Samuel said to Saul, Thou hast done fool-
> ishly: thou hast not kept the commandment of
> the Lord thy God, which he commanded thee:
> for now would the Lord have established thy
> kingdom upon Israel for ever. But now thy king-
> dom shall not continue: the Lord hath sought
> him a man after his own heart, and the Lord hath
> commanded him to be captain over his people,
> because thou hast not kept that which the Lord
> commanded thee."

Saul's impatience cost him his kingship and prevented the throne from passing to his sons. God had already picked Saul's replacement and—did you catch it? It was a man after God's own heart—David, son of Jesse—who had not yet been anointed by Samuel. Saul's inability to be patient ended up costing him the very Spirit of God that was upon him, and the only spirits that would be with him until his death would be those distressing spirits that came to torment him from sleeping (1 Samuel 16:14). Now contrast between Saul's impatience (sandpaper) and the next king, David's patience (silk).

In chapter 16, Samuel is commanded by God to go to Jesse's house, for it was one of Jesse's sons who would be king. When Samuel entered into Jesse's house and told him why he was there, Jesse called all his sons into the house except one. We all know the story: Each son was presented before Samuel, and God rejected each one of them. I can see Samuel scratching his beard and shaking his head, thinking he may have missed hearing God on who was to be king. Yet, he asked Jesse if he had another son somewhere, maybe thinking he had an older son not living at home.

Jesse replied that he had another son, his youngest, who was out watching sheep. Samuel commanded to have him brought, and it is then that the Lord says that this other son is the next King. Samuel then pours the anointing oil upon David's head, declaring him king at the ripe old age of about fifteen. It will be fifteen years before he is king in Judah and another seven before he is king over all of Israel.

However, even before David is king, he becomes a fugitive sought by Saul. From 1 Samuel chapter 18 until the 5th chapter of 2 Samuel, David is a wanted man. Yet, he does not get impatient to inherit the throne. Twice while on the run, God Himself gives David permission to kill Saul and even delivers Saul to him, but David refuses to harm the Lord's anointed. In fact, in 1 Samuel 24, Saul goes into a cave where David and his men were hiding and was so close to him that David was able to cut off a piece of Saul's robe. Then in chapter 26, while Saul slept, David and Abishai sneak into his tent and steal his spear and his water jug. Both times David could have killed Saul but did not, and here's why:

> "And David said to Abishai, Destroy him not:
> for who can stretch forth his hand against the
> Lord 's anointed, and be guiltless? David said
> furthermore, As the Lord liveth, the Lord shall
> smite him; or his day shall come to die; or he

shall descend into battle, and perish. The Lord
forbid that I should stretch forth mine hand
against the Lord' s anointed: but, I pray thee,
take thou now the spear that is at his bolster, and
the cruse of water, and let us go,"
(1 Samuel 26: 9-11).

In verse 10 David explains that Saul will die—whether by
God's own hand, old age, or death in battle—but it will not be
by David's own hand. Subsequently, David was rewarded for
his patience; God promised him that his lineage would never be
removed from the throne (2 Samuel 7:16).

David's patience came through process. He was first a shep-
herd watching his father's flocks. In the field he would feed,
water, watch, heal, and protect the sheep. He became a hero, and
just as quickly an outlaw, hiding from Saul to avoid conflict with
him. He was away from his homeland, away from his countrymen, and away from the places of worship at which he so loved
to be, and yet he learned patience through process, through op-
portunities wherein he restrained himself. He was patient and
willing to wait on the Lord. Even as king, it would be seven
years before all of Israel would accept his kingship. Yet the reward for patience would be the throne forever belonging to his
house (though ultimately Jesus—the King of Kings—would one
day establish His throne in Jerusalem in the house of David).

In addition to the story of David, here are some other examples of patience or longsuffering in the Bible:

- For 120 years Noah built on the ark. In the face of great
  mockery, here was Noah building a boat, in the desert,
  when it had never rained on the earth.

- Job suffered great loss. Though he complained to God to
  show Him where he had sinned, he also endured his trial

and even made a declaration that if he died, he knew he would praise God once again in his flesh.

- Romans 5:3-5: "And not only so, but we glory in tribulations also: knowing that tribulation worketh patience; And patience, experience; and experience, hope: And hope maketh not ashamed; because the love of God is shed abroad in our hearts by the Holy Ghost which is given unto us."

Do you see the process for patience? Patience is learned and practiced through tribulations—troubles! If you ask for patience, get ready for a lot of trouble, because it takes a lot of pain and frustration and testing to change sandpaper to silk!

However, there is a reward. Look for it. It is through our tribulations that we gain experience, and experience gives us hope. Hope is what allows us to transform from sandpaper to silk.

Those people that seem to always get under your skin or drive you up a wall—those other drivers on the road, your children, co-workers, and even family members—are all working to bring you the capacity to accept or tolerate delay, trouble, or suffering without getting angry or upset. This in turn creates a "texture" that draws people to want what is inside you (silk), rather than you "rubbing" them the wrong way like sandpaper.

Points to Ponder

1. How is patience (longsuffering) developed within us?

2. What is the definition of patience? What is the definition of impatience? Which best describes you?

3. What was the difference between David and Saul?

4. Other than Noah and Job, are there other examples from Scripture that show patience and its rewards?

5. How would you describe yourself? Are you sandpaper or are you silk? What circumstances in your life can transform you from sandpaper to silk?

CHAPTER 7
THE TASTE-GENTLENESS

Psalms 34:8
O taste and see that the Lord is good:
blessed is the man that trusteth in him.

Thus far in our study of the fruit of the Spirit, we have learned that the stem, skin, aroma, and texture create an appetite to want the fruit. The stem reaches out, the skin both protects the fruit and shows its ripeness, the aroma creates hunger for what is inside, and the texture confirms its ripeness or maturity. Now we come to the gentleness of the fruit—its taste.

The moment we take that first bite of a grape, biting through its meat, we experience the gentle sweetness of its taste filling of our mouths. At this point, one bite will not satisfy us; it is only when we have devoured that piece of fruit to its core that we feel satisfied and full: "O taste and see that the Lord is good: blessed is the man that trusteth in him," (Psalms 34:8).

One taste and no one can resist if what they are tasting is the fruit from the true vine, Jesus. It seems so simple, and yet for many outside the household of faith, it is not the sweetness of the Holy Spirit they have been given a taste of, but instead the bitter taste of the fruit of judgment, condemnation, and self-righteousness. This sourness causes repulsion and keeps them from wanting a second bite.

The taste they experience should be the sweet taste of salvation and the lingering luscious flavor of God's bountiful grace.

The hunger to know the rich goodness of the Lord will overcome even the hardest of hearts; that first taste will ignite an insatiable desire for more, and it is then that the unrepentant will fall to their knees and in brokenness cry out for more. In so doing, they will experience the fullness that all of that fruit's juicy meat has to offer.

A look into Luke 8:26-40 shows us that when Jesus went into the land of the Gadarenes (also in Matthew 8 and Mark 5), He encountered a demonically possessed man living in the tombs. The man was so overpowered by the many demons within him that he would break chains in two and shatter the fetters that were used to control him. Yet when Jesus was confronted by these demons, He cast them out from the man and into a herd of swine that then ran off a cliff and drowned themselves.

The people of the area came out to see what had happened, and being afraid of Jesus, they begged Him to leave. Jesus, being the gentleman that He was, obliged and entered the boat to go back across to the other side of the sea. But look at what happens in Luke 8:38-40:

> "Now the man out of whom the devils were departed besought him that he might be with him: but Jesus sent him away, saying, Return to thine own house, and shew how great things God hath done unto thee. And he went his way, and published throughout the whole city how great things Jesus had done unto him. And it came to pass, that, when Jesus was returned, the people gladly received him: for they were all waiting for him."

When the man who had been delivered begged Jesus that he might go with Him, Jesus had a better idea. I believe it was with gentleness that He requested this man to stay behind and go and tell how the Lord had shown him great compassion that day. When the man did as Christ asked, it was because he had tasted the goodness of God that day and wanted nothing more than to tell others of the wonderful grace of the Lord. And what was the result of the gentleness of the Lord? "And it came to pass, that, when Jesus was returned, the people gladly received him: for they were all waiting for him," (Luke 8:40). One man's taste of the Lord caused a multitude to become hungry for the Lord as well. The entire region, by the testimony of one man who had tasted and seen that the Lord was good, had a desire to taste all that Jesus had to give.

The Woman at the Well

"The woman saith unto him, Sir, give me this water, that I thirst not, neither come hither to draw. Jesus saith unto her, Go, call thy husband, and come hither. The woman answered and said, I have no husband. Jesus said unto her, Thou hast well said, I have no husband: For thou hast had five husbands; and he whom thou now hast is not thy husband: in that saidst thou truly," (John 4:15-18).

In this conversation, the woman is speaking from the physical realm, and Jesus is speaking from the spiritual realm. As they are conversing, Jesus has created in her a desire to taste what He has. When Jesus says to her that the man she was living with now was not her husband, He did not do so in a manner of judgment or condemnation; He was gently revealing to her who He was. Later, in John 4:28-29, the woman left her water pot and ran into the city to tell them to come and see this man who had told her of all that she had done.

Do you think that if Jesus had told her of her past with an arrogant, condemning attitude that she would have wanted anyone to come hear Him? It was because Jesus gave her a taste of the fruit of the Spirit—the gentle sweet flavor of God's grace—that she wanted everyone to have a taste too.

The Adulterous Woman

"And the scribes and Pharisees brought unto
him a woman taken in adultery; and when they
had set her in the midst, They say unto him,
Master, this woman was taken in adultery, in
the very act. Now Moses in the law commanded
us, that such should be stoned: but what sayest
thou? This they said, tempting him, that they
might have to accuse him. But Jesus stooped
down, and with his finger wrote on the ground,
as though he heard them not. So when they
continued asking him, he lifted up himself, and
said unto them, He that is without sin among
you, let him first cast a stone at her. And again
he stooped down, and wrote on the ground. And
they which heard it, being convicted by their
own conscience, went out one by one, beginning
at the eldest, even unto the last: and Jesus was
left alone, and the woman standing in the midst.
When Jesus had lifted up himself, and saw

none but the woman, he said unto her, Woman,
where are those thine accusers? hath no man
condemned thee? She said, no man, Lord. And
Jesus said unto her, Neither do I condemn thee:
go, and sin no more," (John 8:3-11).

Let's examine the contrast between Jesus and the scribes and
Pharisees. Those men of the law wanted to stone the woman to
death, to condemn her because she had committed adultery. By
their accusations, they were saying that you first have to be clean
to be forgiven. They were shoving the bitter fruit of judgment
and condemnation down her throat with Jesus' permission.

However, in verse 7, look at how Jesus just wrote in the sand
as though He had not heard them. He was not going to be caught
up in some conflict that would destroy His message or His reputation, nor would He be drawn into an attitude of self-righteous
behavior. Jesus told us that His purpose in coming into the world
was to save the world, not condemn it (John 3:17).

Instead, Jesus stood up, and with one simple statement
stopped these men in their tracks. He said that the one without sin may cast the first stone. In other words, who are you to
condemn this woman when you are not pure either? It makes
one wonder what it was He wrote in the sand. Scripture says
that the others were so condemned within their own hearts that
they dropped their stones—from the oldest to the youngest—
and went away.

Then Jesus asked the woman where her accusers were. She
replied there were none, and Jesus said, "Neither do I condemn
thee: go, and sin no more," (John 8:11). Then and there, in the
dusty courtyard of the temple, the woman got a taste of the Lord
and left knowing the gentleness of grace. She tasted and found
the Lord to be good. It is this taste of the fruit we offer those
outside the household of faith that will either leave them want-

ing all of it or cause them to be repulsed and harden their hearts even more to the Gospel.

How do you respond to that drunk on the street? What taste do you offer the drug addict walking down the street who is just skin and bones? What fruit do you offer to the prostitute working the corner? How about a mother who abandons her children to go and live life her way? The abusive husband who leaves his battered and bruised wife weeping on the kitchen floor while he goes out and gets drunk? The child molester, rapist, drug dealer, murderer, or terrorist—what fruit do they receive from us? Is it the bitter fruit of condemnation, judgment, or self-righteousness, or is it the sweet taste of God's good grace?

POINTS TO PONDER

1. What is the purpose of the first four characteristics of the fruit of the Spirit?

2. How does gentleness relate to the taste of a fruit?

3. How did Jesus display gentleness to the Gaderene, the woman at the well, and the adulterous woman?

4. How did others respond to the gentleness displayed by Jesus in the examples above?

5. What is your response to the examples of the different types of people listed at the end of this chapter?

CHAPTER 8
THE MEAT-GOODNESS

Psalm 107:9
For he satisfieth the longing soul, and filleth
the hungry soul with goodness.

The meat of the fruit is what is wrapped within the skin, and it is really what we desire when we take that first bite. It is when we sink our teeth into the fruit and bite through the skin that we experience that first taste of the fruit. However, we do not stop there with just a simple taste; the sweet tender meat behind the skin is what we really want. The meat of the fruit is what fills us up and satisfies our hunger. After a single bite of a cool, crisp apple, it must be consumed to its very core before our desire for it is satisfied. You just can't eat one bite, as the saying goes.

In the sweet crisp meat of the apple are nutrients and fiber that both fill us up and give us strength. Just what are the nutrients (characteristics) of the meat within the apple? There are vitamins, minerals, energy producers, electrolytes, and phyto-nutrients. The chart below shows them as determined by the USDA. No wonder an apple a day keeps the doctor away:

Energy	50 Kcal	2.5%	Lutein-zeaxanthin	29 µg	
Carbohy-drates	13.81 g	11%	Protein	0.26 g	0.5%

Total Fat	0.17 g	0.5%	Cholesterol	0 mg	0%
Dietary Fiber	2.40 g	6%	Folates	3 µg	1%
Niacin	0.091 mg	1%	Pantothenic acid	0.061 mg	1%
Pyridoxine	0.041 mg	3%	Riboflavin	0.026 mg	2%
Thiamin	0.017 mg	1%	Vitamin A	54 IU	2%
Vitamin C	4.6 mg	8%	Vitamin E	0.18 mg	1%
Vitamin K	2.2 µg	2%	Sodium	1 mg	0%
Potassium	107 mg	2%	Calcium	6 mg	0.6%.
Magnesium	5 mg	1%.	Phosphorus	11 mg	2%
Zinc	0.04 mg	0%	Carotene-ß	27 µg	
Crypto-xanthin-ß	11 µg				

As we can see, the "goodness" of the fruit of the Spirit is the meat, because it is the "goodness" of the Lord that fills us according to Psalm 107:9: "For he satisfieth the longing soul, and filleth the hungry soul with goodness." He, the Lord, satisfies the longing soul with goodness.

When we think of the goodness of God, what would be the characteristics of His goodness? Let's list them:

Love	Forgiveness
Mercy	Grace
Faithfulness	Righteousness
Provision	Healing
Peace	Hope
Joy	Kindness

It is no wonder that the goodness of God can fill one's starving soul so completely. When you think of how the Lord's goodness fills and satisfies the empty place within man, is it any wonder that the things of this world only bring a brief moment of satisfaction?

Let's look back at the works of the flesh in Galatians 5:19-21:

Adultery	Idolatry	Emulations	Heresies
Fornication	Witchcraft	Wrath	Murders
Uncleanness	Hatred	Strife	Drunkenness
Lasciviousness	Variance	Seditions	Revellings

Is there any one of the works of the flesh listed above that will satisfy a man's soul, quenching his lust? The answer is emphatically *no*! Look at each of those above (the first four being sexual in nature) and each one more depraved than the next. Adultery leads to the breakdown of a marriage. Fornication, which is simply sex outside of marriage between singles, leads to uncleanness (impure thoughts), which leads to lasciviousness (or shameless unbridled lust).

Can you see the rest of the progression of the works of the flesh? Idolatry is the concept of putting any person, object, or principle before God. The longer the object is held above God, the more it will cause one to practice witchcraft, which we know from the book of 1 Samuel is really the sin of rebellion against God and His commandments. This in turn takes one down dark paths of destruction.

Hatred can never be satisfied; there will always be an object to hate. When the KKK was in its heyday, they didn't only hate blacks and Jews. They also hated Catholics with a passion, even the white ones! Hatred takes one to variance, which is strife and discord that you cause for yourself. Variance takes you into emulation, which in this context means jealousy that brings wrath and rage. Rage then produces strife, which is division or breakdown of the body of Christ, of homes, and of friendships.

As you can see, each level brings one to a deeper perversion, to a lower level of depravity—never satisfying, only driving one deeper and deeper into the pit. Not a single one of those works can satisfy a languishing soul. Not one can change a person into a compassionate, caring, loving person; yet, the goodness of our Lord will fill the starving soul of a man or woman, changing them completely from their fleshly lusts that are driving them to destruction into people filled with His goodness, reaching out to others in love.

The transformational power of God's goodness is best expressed through the interaction between Jesus and Zacchaeus. Zacchaeus was just such a person of depravity when he encountered Jesus and was so transformed that those around him must have been shocked. In the beginning of Luke 19, Zacchaeus is described as a "chief publican," which means he oversaw a number of tax collectors who collected taxes for Rome. In many instances these tax collectors would extort extra "tax" money from people and keep it for themselves; thus, many became rich off the backs of their fellow Jews. These collectors were despised because of their chosen vocation in assisting the Romans and for their dishonesty in their amounts and methods of collections. It is said that Zacchaeus was a rich man but not a devout one.

We all know the story: Zacchaeus, having heard Jesus was in town, wanted to get a glimpse of Him. As the crowds grew, he was unable to see over them because of his rather short stature. So, being an industrious fellow, he ran ahead and climbed a sycamore tree to get a look at Jesus:

> "And when Jesus came to the place, he looked up, and saw him, and said unto him, Zacchaeus, make haste, and come down; for to day I must abide at thy house. And he made haste, and came down, and received him joyfully. And when they saw it, they all murmured, saying, That he was gone to be guest with a man that is a sinner," (Luke 19:5-7).

When Jesus said that He was to dine with Zacchaeus, the people were astonished that Jesus would be the guest of a sinner. Zacchaeus' reputation was well known among the residents of Jericho.

However, the Scripture shows a very different man than the one who climbed the tree to see Jesus after his encounter with the Lord. In Luke 19:6 it says that Zacchaeus received the Lord joyfully, as a changed man. Here was the greatest figure in all of Israel, and this person wanted to have dinner with Zacchaeus. Zacchaeus was filled in an instant with the goodness of God, and look at what it did to his very nature in verse 8: "And Zacchaeus stood, and said unto the Lord; Behold, Lord, the half of my goods I give to the poor; and if I have taken any thing from any man by false accusation, I restore him fourfold."

Zacchaeus promised to give half of his wealth to the poor and even vowed to make restitution to those he had cheated by increasing those payments fourfold. Does this not show the power of God's goodness when it fills a man's soul? What kind of testimony would that be to the people of Jericho who knew Zacchaeus and his unethical business practices? Do you think that maybe he also brought his other collectors in line with his new character? Maybe they got saved too!

Another radically changed person was the Apostle Paul. Before his Damascus road conversion he was a zealot against the early church. It was with his consent that Stephen was stoned in Jerusalem. By his own testimony he was responsible for pouring out immeasurable persecution upon the early church. Yet, when he was drastically changed—not by punishment but by the goodness of the Lord—he became the greatest witness of Jesus Christ the world has ever seen. Even today his writings fill close to two-thirds of the New Testament. Paul was so radically changed that God changed his name, and Paul's greatest concern became care of the churches.

It is the goodness of God that will radically change even the vilest of sinners into the greatest workers of Christ. If we are not filled with the goodness of the Holy Spirit, then we must pray and pray fervently for that goodness to fill every nook and cranny of our souls so that we can then offer to men, women, and children whose souls are languishing unfilled the only thing that cannot only fill them, but nourish them with hope, love, and faith.

POINTS TO PONDER

1. The meat of the fruit satisfies our natural hunger by filling us up. What does the goodness of God fill us with?

2. What other characteristics can you add to the list of God's goodness?

3. Why do the works of the flesh leave some unsatisfied?

4. Which characteristics of the goodness of God had the greatest effect on both Zacchaeus and Paul?

5. Do you find yourself avoiding contact with sinners, or are you like Jesus and search out sinners with whom to share the goodness of God?

CHAPTER 9
THE CORE-FAITH

Hebrews 11:1
Now faith is the substance of things hoped for,
the evidence of things not yet seen.

The core (faith) of a fruit is the foundation upon which all other traits are built, and it is what holds the fruit together. The stem (love) is its anchor and the pipeline that pumps life into the fruit, but the very life and every attribute of the fruit comes from the core

Look at a fruit such as a grape. Where does the stem go? The stem (love) extends from the branch and disappears into the core (faith). From that core comes the skin (joy)—it's strength—and then comes its aroma (peace), which progresses into its texture (patience), then builds to its taste (gentleness), thereby producing its meat (goodness), then meekness (the juice), and then temperance (the seed).

Still, each is dependent on the foundation of faith: "But without faith it is impossible to please him: for he that cometh to God must believe that he is, and that he is a rewarder of them that diligently seek him," (Hebrews 11:6). We must believe that God is who He says He is. We must be convinced that He is eternal. We must be convinced that He is sovereign. We must be convinced that He is omnipotent. We must be convinced that He will reward those who diligently seek Him. Faith is central to all that we as Christians believe, and without faith it is impossible to please God! How can we believe who God is without faith?

The writer of Hebrews goes on to say, "Through faith we understand that the worlds were framed by the word of God, so that things which are seen were not made of things which do appear," (11:3). It takes faith to understand creation and how the world was formed, but what exactly is faith? The definition of faith in Hebrews 11:1 is "the substance of things hoped for, the evidence of things not yet seen." This one verse is used as the complete definition of faith, yet oftentimes it is just a Christian cliché and many do not understand its meaning. Have you tried to break down this Scripture into its simplest form? Have you tried to explain what exactly this verse of Scripture is saying? It's not an easy thing to do, even for the greatest of scholars. Let's try breaking it down here, because without the understanding of faith, how can one truly have it?

Let's look to another definition. Faith, as defined by *Strong's Exhaustive Concordance*, is "persuasion in or conviction of a moral truth," and substance is a "thing put under, substructure, foundation." Put together, *Strong's* is telling us that when we have faith, we are completely convinced of a moral truth—or we are completely convinced that the Lord is who He says He is— and that faith is the very foundation of those things for which we hope.

What are those things we hope for? Salvation, eternal life, power over temptation, wisdom, understanding God's truth, power to minister to others, and a longer list that cannot be elaborated here. Our foundation is that we are convinced of a moral truth, that if God said He would save us- then He has, and that if God said He would give us eternal life, then we are convinced He has and that He will.

The foundation of our lives is the fact that we are convinced of all that the Lord said He would do. Period. But what is the proof—the evidence—of those things not yet seen? The proof is living our lives in the fullness of our convictions. And what are those convictions? If you continually question your salvation, then you are not convinced that Jesus has the ability to forgive your sins. If you question whether you will go to heaven, then you are not convinced that Jesus has the ability to give eternal life. If you question that Jesus can give you power over temptation, then you really don't believe that Jesus has power over temptation.

Without a convinced heart, would we be willing to share our testimony with a stranger? Without a convinced heart, could we pray for a lost soul or for someone's healing? Are we truly convinced in our hearts that Jesus will—as we lay hands upon the sick—touch them and heal them? Or are we more convinced by doubt and fear? As love urges us to reach beyond ourselves to the world, it is the firm conviction that God is who He says He is that gives us the courage to go forward and share his love.

Look at all of the attributes of the fruit of the Spirit that we have learned about thus far. How many can manifest in our lives without faith? Love (the stem) anchors us to the vine and our fruit to the branch (ourselves). Yet it is faith (the core) that will bring the fruit. What is it we are hoping for? Our hope is that our fruit will draw others to Christ, and our hope is that our fruit gives us our true identity, which is Christ. Our faith—our firm conviction—is the foundation that proves those things not seen. Moreover, faith is not just something one has; it also produces action. Let's look at just a few examples of heroes of faith in Hebrews 11:

- Abel, it says, offered a better sacrifice by faith. Why? Because he had a firm conviction of what was right.

- By faith, Noah preached that the world would be flooded and built a boat to save his family and the animals. Why? Because he had a firm conviction that God would flood the earth.

- By faith, Abraham packed his family and all he had and

moved to a strange land. Why? Because he had a firm conviction that the Lord was truthful and would do what He said He would do.

- Moses went to Pharaoh to deliver the children of Israel out of bondage. Why? Because he had a firm conviction that God would deliver them from Pharaoh.

Each one of those people mentioned above had faith, and their faith produced action. James wrote in chapter 2 of the book that bears his name, "Even so faith, if it hath not works, is dead, being alone. Yea, a man may say, Thou hast faith, and I have works: shew me thy faith without thy works, and I will shew thee my faith by my works." James knew that faith produces works because it creates action on the part of the believer. He was saying that there are those who say, "I have faith," but are not active in their faith. According to James, their faith is dead. James says that he will demonstrate his faith in the name of Jesus, by his works, such as witnessing, prayers of faith for others in the name of Jesus, and by his care of the poor and lonely.

How can faith as action affect others and us? Let's look at Acts chapter 3:

> "Now Peter and John went up together into the temple at the hour of prayer, being the ninth hour. And a certain man lame from his mother's womb was carried, whom they laid daily at the gate of the temple which is called Beautiful, to ask alms of them that entered into the temple; Who seeing Peter and John about to go into the temple asked an alms. And Peter, fastening his eyes upon him with John, said, Look on us. And he gave heed unto them, expecting to receive something of them. Then Peter said, Silver and gold have I none; but such as I have give I thee: In the name

of Jesus Christ of Nazareth rise up and walk. And he took him by the right hand, and lifted him up: and immediately his feet and ankle bones received strength. And he leaping up stood, and walked, and entered with them into the temple, walking, and leaping, and praising God."

Now, whose faith made that man whole? Was it the faith of the lame man, or was it Peter and John's faith that made him whole? Let it sink in for a second. It was John and Peter's faith in Jesus that brought healing to this man. As Peter told the crowd that gathered when they entered the temple in verse 16, "And his (Jesus) name through faith in his (Jesus) name hath made this man strong, whom ye see and know: yea, the faith which is by him (Jesus) hath given him this perfect soundness in the presence of you all." (emphasis mine)

As we see, it was the firm conviction (faith) that Jesus (who was God in the flesh Immanuel) would heal this man's legs when Peter looked at the man and prayed. Peter was not in fear of failure because his faith was actively producing works that pointed to Jesus and confirmed the testimony of Jesus Christ.

There are too many timid Christians in the United States who are afraid to exercise true faith; thus, their faith has no life. If the core of a fruit becomes weak or diseased, the fruit will die on the branch. Our core must continually be nourished through active faith or it will become weak and diseased and no longer have life. As James put it, our faith will be dead.

It is only when we are convinced—firmly and unwaveringly convinced—that the Lord will follow through on His promises that we are then prepared to offer our fruit to the world, and subsequently that the world will identify us with our true vine—the Lord Jesus Christ.

So, what is the condition of the core of your fruit?

POINTS TO PONDER

1. If the stem of the fruit of the Spirit is the support for the fruit, what is the core to the fruit?

2. What is the foundation of your life?

3. What is the evidence in your life that reveals your conviction that God is who He says He is?

4. James says that faith without works is dead. How is faith active in your life?

5. What actions did Peter perform that proved his faith in Jesus in Acts 3:1-8?

CHAPTER 10
THE JUICE-MEEKNESS

Galatians 6:1
Brethren, if a man be overtaken in a fault, ye which
are spiritual, restore such an one in the spirit of meekness;
considering thyself, lest thou also be tempted.

It is 2:00 a.m. and the small infant begins to stir in his bed. As he wakes up he begins to cry because he is hungry and needs to be fed. The mother quickly responds to her baby's cry and runs to gather him into her arms as she reaches quickly into her refrigerator, drawing out an apple and placing it into the crib along with her baby. The child continues to cry for a while longer, exhausts itself, and goes back to sleep. A few hours later he awakens crying, and Mom runs to see what is the matter, and once again places the apple into his hands saying, "Here, eat. It will be okay."

The child continues to sleep as he exhausts himself until one of two things happen: either the child will die of starvation within a week while the apple rots beside him, or the mother will reach in and give him a bottle of apple juice, which will nourish him and strengthen him.

The juice of a fruit has all the strength of the meat, yet it is easier to swallow and digest. We know there isn't a mother in the world who would believe her infant child could digest— much less eat—an apple. Yet, if she were to squeeze that apple and strain the juice and then give it to her baby, then that child could enjoy not only the taste, but also experience the goodness of the fruit.

Many people define this juice—meekness—as weakness. In reality, meekness is strength under control. A father and his daughter with whom I recently attended church illustrate this point well. Caitlyn, the daughter was this dainty little thing, all of four foot three inches and topping the scales at a whopping 58 pounds. The father Will, in contrast, was six foot three inches and tipped the scales at a diminutive 230 pounds. When the daughter stood in front of her father and he placed his huge hands on her shoulders, they covered most of her chest.

As a father, he had the responsibility of disciplining his daughter when she disobeyed. Can you imagine the damage he could inflict on her if he did not restrain or control his strength? If he was to unleash all of his strength when disciplining his little girl, he could seriously injure or even kill her. Therefore, he controls his strength so as not to harm her; he knows that discipline should be instructive, not destructive.

Conversely, we have all seen what happens when men obtain great power and rule without restraint. Lord Acton said, "Power tends to corrupt and absolute power corrupts absolutely," and history has provided us with far too many examples. There were the Roman Caesars who declared themselves gods and were perhaps some of the most brutal of all monarchs. In our modern history we have seen such despots as Hitler, Stalin, Mao, Sadaam Hussein, and even the current dictator of Syria, Bashar al-Assad. They have not only ruled the people of their countries with iron fists, but have also thumbed their noses at the world as well. While these examples mostly draw on actions towards others, meekness actually deals with a believer's inward character rather than his outward actions. As such, meekness is best utilized with believers under three conditions. The first is when one is teaching new followers or believers of Christ the doctrines of faith. The second is when believers are under great tribulation or in the midst of a hard battle. The last lies in disciplining those of the household of God when they have stumbled and fallen into temptations.

Let us first examine how meekness is used in bringing spiritual maturity to a new believer. There are two distinct descriptions of the Word of God as food. The first is described as "meat" and the other is described as "milk." We know that both steak (meat) and milk come from the same source—the cow. Infants are given milk for nourishment while an adult enjoys steak. Both milk and meat contain the same nutrients, just as the meat and juice of the fruit contain the same benefits.

New believers are just like newly born infants; their knowledge of God and His doctrines is limited. Therefore, it would be hard for them to understand the book of Revelation when they don't yet understand the doctrines of water baptism, sanctification, baptism in the Holy Ghost, or other doctrines that will get their faith growing. What they need is not the meat of the word, but the milk—the simple truths that are foundational to their faith. Teaching them to pray, to take time reading the Word, and finding the simplest answers when a question arises are key.

We see an example of this type of meekness in 1 Corinthians in which Paul writes a harsh letter to the church to set the people in order. He tells the believers in Corinth that they were like children still thinking in the flesh, needing to be put in order:

> "And I, brethren, could not speak unto you as
> unto spiritual, but as unto carnal, even as unto
> babes in Christ. I have fed you with milk, and
> not with meat: for hitherto ye were not able
> to bear it, neither yet now are ye able. For ye
> are yet carnal: for whereas there is among you
> envying, and strife, and divisions, are ye not
> carnal, and walk as men?" (1 Corinthians 3:1-3).

Here Paul begins to instruct this group of new believers in their worship, personal lives, and church leadership. Paul was instructing them in all areas of faith, especially how to live their lives as an example of Christ to those in the area around them. These believers were not ready for deep, spiritual truths and needed to grasp simplistic instructions that would allow them to grow into mature Christians.

Peter, however, wrote to a different group of new believers—those in the area of what is now modern-day Turkey. During this time the Christians were under great persecution and the believers there needed to be encouraged. As new believers, Peter encouraged them to look to the pure spiritual "milk" so that they could grow easily in their salvation (1 Peter 2:1-3).

Secondly, meekness is also best utilized when we are in battle or in the midst of a storm. These are times during which we need to hear that God's love for us is so strong that we cannot be separated from it. (Romans 8:35-39). Many times in life we need to go back to the pure milk of the Word rather than the meat to regain our strength. Even in our physical bodies there are times when meat makes us sicker or cannot be digested properly, and it is then that we turn to juice or milk in order to be sustained and regain strength.

Thirdly, we especially need meekness when dealing with a believer that has fallen into temptation and is overtaken by sin. Paul instructed us in Galatians 6: 1,"Brethren, if a man be overtaken in a fault, ye which are spiritual, restore such an one in the spirit of meekness; considering thyself, lest thou also be tempted." The key word in that verse is "meekness."

How many times have we heard this: "I don't go to church because they think they are so holy," or "I quit going to church because I messed up once and they treated me like I had a disease," or "Why should I go to church? All they do is tell me that what I am doing wrong."

The holier-than-thou attitude has caused more souls to perish than I believe any other work of Satan. The Apostle Paul, when bringing up the subject of fallen brethren, made sure to instruct that one should be reconciled to Christ through the spirit of meekness. As believers, it is a lot easier to condemn than it is to get our hands dirty by reaching down to those who have fallen. When someone has fallen they need the juice of the fruit of the Spirit; their hearts and minds are not ready for the meat. They need reconciliation. They need to hear of God's unfailing grace. They need to be loved and encouraged to return to Christ, and it must be in meekness.

It is scriptures like 1 John 1:9 that says,"If we confess our sins (to God), he is faithful and just to forgive us our sins, and to cleanse us from all unrighteousness", and Psalm 51, which David wrote after his affair with Bathsheba, that is the juice that brings reconciliation. These Scriptures are life-saving juice to a fallen brother or sister. It is in meekness that we have the greatest opportunity to see someone restored to the household of faith.

"And the Lord said, Simon, Simon, behold, Satan hath desired to have you, that he may sift you as wheat: But I have prayed for thee, that thy faith fail not: and when thou art converted, strengthen thy brethren," (Luke 22:31-32). Jesus—after instituting the Lord's Supper—turns to Peter and says that Satan has asked Him to sift Peter like wheat. That has to be the one of the most discouraging things ever spoken to someone by the Lord. Imagine you are Peter: You have spent the past three and a half years following Jesus. You have given up everything to be with Him—career, family time, money—and for your devotion and dedication the one you followed looks at you and says that the devil has asked permission to have at you, and from His tone is given permission to do just that.

However, Jesus did not leave him stranded. He did not leave Peter to face this test alone. Jesus followed it up with very strong words of encouragement and strength: Don't worry. I have already prayed for you that your faith not fail. After you come through this time of testing, strengthen your brethren.

Peter was heading into one of the toughest challenges of his newfound faith. There in the upper room, before Peter was to enter this trial of his faith, Jesus used meekness to encourage him. And when Jesus turned and looked Peter in the eye with meekness, after that third denial of Him, that gave Peter strength to move beyond his failure and to become the strong leader that the early church needed in order to survive the harsh persecution that would come.

There are many times that we similarly need to offer the juice of the fruit of the Spirit to those around us. They may be new babies in Christ not quite ready for the meat of the Word. There are the fallen that need the juice of the fruit to restore faith in their lives when a hard word will only drive them further into despair. There are still those who are wounded in battle, and because they are weakened from the fight, they may need the juice for a short season to gain the strength to return to the fight and show forth the power of God's truth. The juice (meekness) of the fruit of the Spirit has all the strength that the meat (goodness) has, but at certain times it is the best way to minister the truth of God's word.

POINTS TO PONDER

1. The juice of a fruit has all the same nutrients as the meat. "Meekness" shares characteristics with what other part of the fruit of the Spirit?

2. What is the definition of meekness?

3. What is the best way to restore a brother or sister to the faith?

4. What are the three conditions under which "meekness" is best utilized with believers?

5. Have you experienced any of the three conditions when you needed milk? What did you learn from your experience?

CHAPTER 11
THE SEED-TEMPERANCE

2 Peter 1:5-6
Add to your faith virtue; and to virtue knowledge;
and to knowledge temperance; and to temperance patience;
and to patience godliness.

The seed of the fruit of the Spirit is temperance, or self-control, the virtue of one who masters his desires and passions, especially his sensual appetites. The ability to master one's passions and desires comes through the implanting of the Word into his heart. It is through the Word taking root within the life of a believer that the ability to control one's passions and desires is developed.

Look at a fruit when it is cut in half. The core is built around the seed. I know that when we study faith we discover that it is the core and everything was built upon it (with the exception of love—the stem). But faith must come from something. The Bible says in Romans 10:17, "So then faith cometh by hearing, and hearing by the word of God." For us to have faith we must first have our ears opened, and it is the Word of God that opens them. It is the Word, once received into our hearts, that reveals the very first thing that needs to be brought under control—our sinful hearts. Once faith is birthed into our lives and we repent for our sins, God then cleanses us from our sins and we are born again. It takes the Word implanted within our soul to ignite faith, and then it begins a journey to destroy the lusts of the flesh through the development of temperance within our hearts.

A lack of temperance in a believer's life is more destructive to the Gospel than a lack of faith. Without temperance, the believer's testimony of the power of the Gospel to change a life becomes a lie because they will continue to live in the flesh, always looking to their desires to be fulfilled rather than desire the will of God to rule them.

The Apostle Paul helps illustrate this point in Philippians when he wrote about worldly Christians: "Brethren, be followers together of me, and mark them which walk so as ye have us for an ensample. (For many walk, of whom I have told you often, and now tell you even weeping, that they are the enemies of the cross of Christ: Whose end is destruction, whose God is their belly, and whose glory is in their shame, who mind earthly things)," (Philippians 3:17-19).

Paul was encouraging the believers to follow his example and travel their journey of faith in the same manner as he. He also explained that there were those among them whose end would be destruction because they were looking only to have their fleshly lusts fulfilled, that their bellies were their God. This brought Paul to tears.

Similarly, the lack of focus in churches today may have also brought Paul to tears. How many people today sit in a church service not focused on the presence of the Lord, not worshipping Him in spirit and truth, instead just thinking about where they will eat afterwards and who they will invite to come with them? How many people are bound by something so strong that they cannot lay it down for just a few hours and focus on the Lord and what He wants to do? How many people come into church and sit there thinking about what everybody else has and how it isn't fair that they don't have those things? How many come into the church wanting to be blessed rather than to be a blessing to others?

Paul wrote about himself (and to us) in 1 Corinthians 9:27: "But I keep under my body, and bring it into subjection: lest that by any means, when I have preached to others, I myself should be a castaway." Paul is saying that he must keep his body and the lusts that the physical man desires under subjection. His reasoning was that he would be disqualified to preach the Gospel.

How did he subject himself? By "casting down imaginations, and every high thing that exalteth itself against the knowledge of God, and bringing into captivity every thought to the obedience of Christ," (2 Corinthians 10:5). Paul brought everything under subjection that would try to overcome the knowledge of God by being obedient to Christ! There is that word "knowledge," and knowledge to overcome sin and the flesh comes by the Word, the seed. We can also look to the actions of Jesus in Matthew 4:1-11 that describes the temptation of Christ when He was in the wilderness. How did Jesus fight temptation? He battled temptation with the Word! When He was tempted to turn stones to bread, He answered, "Man does not live by bread alone but by every word that issues from the mouth of God." When Satan came back with the Word, he told Jesus to cast Himself off the pinnacle of the temple because the Word said that angels would protect Him. Jesus answered back with the Word: "Thou shall not tempt The Lord your God." When offered all the kingdoms of this world if He would only bow down and worship Satan, Jesus said, "Get thee hence for it is written thou shalt worship The Lord thy God and him only." All three times Jesus used the Word to battle temptation, and His resistance lay in his temperance developed by the implanted Word.

The implanted Word—the seed—is a living organism. In order for it to release the life within, it must first be planted, and it must then die in order to live. When you see the seed inside a piece of fruit, do you ever envision the vine or tree within the seed? Do you see all of the fruit that will be produced by that seed? The Word—when sown within our lives—causes death, but it is through the death of our old man of sin that the Word is able to take root and live within us, bringing forth fruit.

Peter wrote the following in his second Epistle:

> "And beside this, giving all diligence, add to your faith virtue; and to virtue knowledge; And to knowledge temperance; and to temperance patience; and to patience godliness; And to godliness brotherly kindness; and to brotherly kindness charity. For if these things be in you, and abound, they make you that ye shall neither be barren nor unfruitful in the knowledge of our Lord Jesus Christ," (2 Peter 1:5-8).

Do you see how knowledge comes before temperance? It is imperative that we, as believers, build a life of self-control so that we are not unfruitful in our knowledge of our Lord, Jesus Christ. Our knowledge is found within the Holy Scriptures, and it is the Word—when we allow it—that will change our thoughts and attitudes and bring them in line with His.

There are three areas of our lives that affect our growth in the faith more than any others which demand self-control:

1) Sexual desires

Jesus taught us that to just look at someone with lust was the same as going to bed with them (and this is in the New Testament). For many Christians, the desire to be with someone other than their spouse would be unthinkable; yet, within the Christian community the increase in the number of marriages being destroyed because of pornography is devastating. A lack of self-control sends one down a slippery slope of destruction, and when it happens, how many others are brought down when brother so-and-so is exposed?

Paul wrote to the Corinthian church about sexual sin: "Flee fornication. Every sin that a man doeth is without the body; but he that committeth fornication sinneth against his own body. What? Know ye not that your body is the temple of the Holy Ghost which is in you, which ye have of God, and ye are not your own? For ye are bought with a price: therefore glorify God in your body, and in your spirit, which are God's," (1 Corinthians 6:18-20).

2) Our bellies or fleshly desires (other than sexual)

There are other appetites or fleshly desires that hold many believers prisoner. As we examine ourselves, is there something we have to have so badly that we cannot lay it down for a few hours a week? What one thing will you admit to yourself that has a hold on you so strongly that you could not set it aside for a week? I have to admit that as I began writing this part of the study I failed in a fast that I was on and have had to repent to God and to my wife for my failure. Food is a powerful substance for many people. Yet there are other things that are just as powerful and can have a stranglehold on a believer's life just as strongly as food can.

3) Our loose tongues

You have heard the phrase "loose lips sink ships." Well, a loose tongue can destroy lives. Look at how many Biblical passages are about what comes out of our mouths—filthy communication, lying, blasphemy, and malice!

- James said in James 3 that the tongue, though small, defiles the whole body.

- Jesus said that it is not what goes into our bodies that defiles us but what comes out of our mouths that does

(Matthew 15:11).

- Paul also wrote to the Colossians: "But now ye also put off all these; anger, wrath, malice, blasphemy, filthy communication out of your mouth. Lie not one to another, seeing that ye have put off the old man with his deeds," (Colossians 3:8).

- In Proverbs 21:23 it says, "Whoso keepeth his mouth and his tongue keepeth his soul from troubles." How many times have we regretted something we have said in anger? How many times have we wished we had not said something that was hurtful? How many times have we been the victim of someone's tongue and we can still feel the sting of it today? Sometimes it is better to bite our tongues than to open our mouths and start a whole bunch of trouble.

Temperance, in these areas and others, comes by allowing the Word of God to change us. Charles Stanley once said, "There are too many people in the church today who filter the Word of God through their lives when they should be filtering their lives through the Word of God." The Word will change our whole lives if we sift our lives through it. It can only change us if we allow it to, and as the Word changes us, then temperance will rule us rather than our ungodly desires and passions.

The Christian life is a life of disciplined behavior, and one who can control his flesh and the desires of the flesh will produce life and sow seeds of life in others' lives. Self-control is vital to our testimony, especially when we are out in the world among those who are lost. And it is the seed that is in the center of the core that will reproduce the very fruit of the Spirit in others' lives.

POINTS TO PONDER

1. How does temperance (self-control) represent the seed?

2. What must come before faith?

3. What is the definition of temperance?

4. What three areas of our lives need to be controlled the most?

5. In what areas of your life do you need to work on temperance?

CHAPTER 12
FINAL THOUGHTS

Through this study on the fruit of the Spirit, we have discovered and learned the character and nature of the Holy Spirit. We have also discovered that this is how Jesus is revealed to the world—through us—by the Holy Spirit.

We must remember that you have to have a grape before you have wine. Thus, you must produce the fruit of the Spirit before you operate in its gifts. Just as the wine is the gift from the fruit, so also are the gifts of the Spirit a product of the fruit. Exposing the mature fruit to those in the world will create a hunger for what thrives within fruit.

The one final thought of this study is this: The true sign of the baptism of the Holy Spirit in someone's life is not the gifts operating in their lives, but instead it is the presence of the mature fruit of the Spirit. How they demonstrate the fruit of the Spirit in their lives proves not only if they are filled with the Spirit, but also if they have been immersed within it—if they have truly experienced a change in the very nature of their character and truly walk in the Spirit.